TREESOFHOPE

I Have The Power To Shout Out: A Children's Guide On Body Safety

Copyright © 2021 by Trees of Hope

Published by Trees of Hope
3901 West Broward Blvd., #122195,
Fort Lauderdale, FL 33312

Email booksales@treesofhope.org for any further information about Trees of Hope or for bulk orders or any special requests.

All rights reserved. No part of this publication may be reproduced, stored in or introduced into a retrieval system, or transmitted, in any form, or by any means (electrical, mechanical, photocopying, recording, or otherwise) without the prior written permission of the publisher. Any person who does any unauthorized act in relation to this publication may be liable to criminal prosecution and civil claims for damages.

Cover and interior design: Deja Sessa

First printing 2021

Print ISBN: 978-1-7367546-3-4

LIBRARY OF CONGRESS PUBLISHER'S CATALOGING-IN-PUBLICATION DATA

Names: Zayas, Didi, author. | Sessa, Deja, designer.

Title: *I have the power to shout out: a children's guide on body safety* / written by Didi Zayas; designed by Deja Sessa.

Description: Fort Lauderdale, FL: Trees of Hope, [2021] |

Identifiers: ISBN: 978-1-7367546-3-4

Subjects: LCSH: Child sexual abuse--Prevention. | Child sexual abuse--Prevention--Study and teaching (Preschool) | Touch--Moral and ethical aspects--Study and teaching (Preschool) | Situational awareness--Study and teaching (Preschool) | Intuition--Study and teaching (Preschool) | Danger perception--Study and teaching (Preschool) | Self-confidence--Study and teaching (Preschool) | Self-reliance--Study and teaching (Preschool) | Child molesters--Identification. | Online sexual predators--Identification. | Child welfare.

Classification: LCC: HV6570 .Z39 2021 | DDC: 362.76--dc23

A CHILDREN'S GUIDE ON BODY SAFETY

WRITTEN BY DIDI ZAYAS
DESIGNED BY DEJA SESSA

PUBLISHED BY
TREESOFHOPE

DEAR PARENTS,

Thank you for sharing this important book with your child! It's critical that all children are empowered to **SHOUT OUT** about situations that make them uncomfortable. One of the most common and most effective tactics abusers use is to isolate and silence children.

We understand that talking about sexual abuse with children can be challenging and often feels embarrassing or awkward. **THE PREVENTION IS POSSIBLE** series is designed to not only empower your children but also to empower you.

Throughout this book, you will find a shield symbol like the one below. This symbol lets you know when to go **POWER UP** by going to the **POWER UP PARENT GUIDE** that accompanies the corresponding book in the series. In each, You will find discussion helps, strategies, and ideas for interacting with your children on specific topics that your child is learning about in the books.

Remember, you are your child's most important teacher. Working together, prevention of sexual abuse is possible!

YOUR PRIVATE PARTS ARE YOUR BODY PARTS THAT ARE COVERED BY A BATHING SUIT. THEY ARE SPECIAL, JUST LIKE YOU! YOU CAN ASK YOUR PARENTS OR A TRUSTED ADULT WHAT TO CALL THEM.

IF SOMEONE TELLS YOU TO CALL YOUR PRIVATE PARTS A DIFFERENT NAME THAN THE NAME MOMMY OR DADDY GIVES THEM, YOU SHOULD **SHOUT OUT, GET OUT, AND SAY IT WITH US ...**

GET OUT

"YOUR HEART ALARM MIGHT SHOUT OUT BY MAKING YOU FEEL...

YUCKY	WORRIED	LONELY	SCARED	SWEATY

OR IT MIGHT MAKE YOU HAVE AN UPSET TUMMY. ALWAYS TRUST YOUR HEART ALARM. IF IT SHOUTS OUT, YOU KNOW WHAT TO DO. LET'S SAY IT TOGETHER ..."

SHOUT GET SPEAK

SHOUT OUT

GET OUT

SPEAK OUT

Made in the USA
Columbia, SC
20 March 2025